# THE BATMAN STRIKES! ®

Raintree is an imprint of Capstone Global Library
Limited, a company incorporated in England and
Wales having its registered office at 7 Pilgrim
Street, London, EC4V 6LB - Registered company
number: 6695582

First published by Raintree in 2014
The moral rights of the proprietor have been
asserted.

Ashley C. Andersen Zantop *Publisher*
Michael Dahl *Editorial Director*
Sean Tulien *Editor*
Heather Kindseth *Creative Director*
Bob Lentz *Designer*
Tori Abraham *Production Specialist*

*DC COMICS*
Joan Hilty & Harvey Richards *Original U.S. Editors*
Jeff Matsuda & Dave McCaig *Cover Artists*

ISBN 978 1 406 28566 6

Printed in China.
18 17 16 15 14
10 9 8 7 6 5 4 3 2 1

British Library Cataloguing in Publication Data
A full catalogue record for this book is available
from the British Library.

# CATWOMAN GETS BUSTED BY THE BATMAN

BILL MATHENY .........................................WRITER
CHRISTOPHER JONES ...........................PENCILLER
TERRY BEATTY.......................................INKER
HEROIC AGE...........................................COLOURIST
PAT BROSSEAU ....................................LETTERER

BATMAN CREATED BY
BOB KANE

DING

SO, LET'S TALK ABOUT *US!*

THERE IS NO "US."

FSSSHHH

THEY SNAPPED THE CABLE.

OH POOH. AND I THOUGHT THAT YOU WERE FALLING FOR ME.

SSSSST

CHUD

PFAF

KLANK

HURRY UP. THERE COULD BE TROUBLE.

YIN, *LOOK!*

MILLER FRANKLIN WAS UPSET BY TONIGHT'S *DISAPPEARANCE.* I HAVEN'T HEARD LANGUAGE LIKE THAT SINCE MY MILITARY DAYS.

I'VE GOT MY EYE ON MILLER FRANKLIN. HE'S CREATING AND SELLING *ILLEGAL WEAPONS.*

*CATWOMAN!*

REALLY? YOU THINK SO OR YOU KNOW SO?

I KNOW SO. I JUST HAVEN'T BEEN ABLE TO PROVE IT YET.

INTERESTING. *SAWDUST.* FROM THE SHOE OF ONE OF THE PERPS.

I RECORDED OUR DETECTIVE YIN BEING INTERVIEWED ON TV. APPARENTLY YOUR FELINE FRIEND *STOLE* THE NOVICK DIAMOND.

Det. Ellen Yin. GCPD

Franklin Systems present

NO, SHE TRIED, BUT THE BURGLARS TOOK IT. THEY WERE TRAINED ATHLETES. ONE OF THEM SPOKE FRENCH.

FREEZE THAT FRAME, ALFRED!

CIRQUE DU PARIS? I FAIL TO SEE...

Franklin Systems
presents:
Cirque du Paris

IT'S PRESENTED BY FRANKLIN SYSTEMS. *MILLER* FRANKLIN SYSTEMS! LOOKS LIKE IT'S BOYS' NIGHT OUT TOMORROW, ALFRED.

AND WHERE, MIGHT I ASK, ARE WE GOING?

TO THE CIRCUS.

THE *NERVE* OF THE GOTHAM POLICE DEPARTMENT, SWEETIES!

14

RATHER ENTERTAINING, MASTER BRUCE. I CAN'T RECALL THE LAST TIME WE ATTENDED A CIRCUS.

TWENTY YEARS AGO. WE WENT WITH MY PARENTS.

I'M *SORRY*, MASTER BRUCE. I FORGOT...

DON'T WORRY ABOUT IT.

"IT'S TIME FOR ME TO GO TO WORK.

☐ × 65

YOU *ARE?* WHAT WOULD YOU LIKE *ME* TO DO?

HAVE SOME *POPCORN* AND ENJOY THE SHOW.

# CREATORS

## BILL MATHENY WRITER

Along with comics such as THE BATMAN STRIKES, Bill Matheny has written for TV series including KRYPTO THE SUPERDOG, WHERE'S WALDO, A PUP NAMED SCOOBY-DOO, and many others.

## CHRISTOPHER JONES PENCILLER

Christopher Jones is an artist who has worked for DC Comics, Image, Malibu, Caliber, and Sundragon Comics.

## TERRY BEATTY INKER

Terry Beatty has inked THE BATMAN STRIKES! and BATMAN: THE BRAVE AND THE BOLD as well as several other DC Comics graphic novels.

# GLOSSARY

**accusing**   saying that someone is guilty of something, usually a crime

**chariot**   a carriage with two wheels that was pulled by horses in battle in ancient times

**deadbolt**   a lock with a heavy sliding bar that is moved by turning a knob or key

**flank**   the right or left side of a military formation

**impressive**   deserving attention, admiration, or respect

**passé**   no longer fashionable or popular

**perimeter**   the outside area of a surface

**prowl**   to move quietly through an area while hunting

**testy**   irritable or easily annoyed

**titanium**   a very strong and light silvery metal

# VISUAL QUESTIONS & PROMPTS

**1.** What does this watch do? Why does Bruce Wayne keep it on him at all times?

**2.** Why did the comic book's creators insert a photo in the panel below? How do the two panels relate to each other? [From page 16.]

**3.** Describe in your own words the path that Catwoman travels in the single planel below. What other ways could the comic's creators have shown the path she traveled?

**4.** Why do Catwoman and Batman's bodies overlap the panel borders? Why do you think the comic's creators decided to do this?